Something to share
communicating the good news

NICK FAWCETT

kevin
mayhew

First published in 2002 by
KEVIN MAYHEW LTD
Buxhall, Stowmarket, Suffolk IP14 3BW
Email: info@kevinmayhewltd.com

9 8 7 6 5 4 3 2 1 0

ISBN 1 84003 917 5
Catalogue No 1500509

Cover design by Angela Selfe
Edited by Katherine Laidler
Typesetting by Louise Selfe
Printed and bound in Great Britain

Contents

To Revd Elsie Howell
with thanks for your faithful support,
constant encouragement
and valued friendship

Acknowledgements

The publishers wish to express their gratitude to the following for permission to include copyright material in this book:

The Friends of York Minster, Church House, Ogleforth, York, YO1 7JN, for the prayer 'Grant, O Lord, that none may love you less' by Eric Milner-White, © Friends of York Minster.

The National Council of Teachers of English, 1111 West Kenyon Road, Urbana, IL 61801-1096, USA, for 'What If an Educator Had Written "The Lord's Prayer"' by Tom Dodge, © 1971 the National Council of Teachers of English.

Bible quotations are taken from the New Revised Standard Version of the Bible, copyright © 1989 by the Division of Christian Education of the National Council of the Churches of Christ in the USA. Used by permission. All rights reserved.

Introduction

When the 1990s were designated a decade of evangelism, I couldn't help but have mixed feelings. I applauded the idea of sharing our faith, for this is central to Christian commitment, but I had, and continue to have, reservations as to how this is sometimes done. When I see someone parading a billboard, or standing on a soapbox haranguing passers-by, I can scarcely suppress a groan of despair. Such people, for all their undoubted good intentions, seem to me to do inestimable damage to the public perception of Christianity. Similarly, I cannot warm to the idea of knocking on doors to spread the gospel. Not only has this approach been forever discredited in the minds of many by the efforts of more extreme sectarian groups, but to me it also lacks credibility, smacking more of an attempt to fill our empty pews than of any genuine concern for people. Even evangelistic crusades cause me more than a little unease, notwithstanding the fact that I made my first public confession of faith at a Dick Saunders 'Way to Life' crusade. Many undoubtedly come to faith via this route, but many others make responses in the excitement of the moment, only to lose interest and feel they have tried Christianity and found it wanting.

All this is not to say, of course, that God cannot work through such means or in any other way he chooses, but I have long been convinced that the most meaningful and powerful witness arises in the context of day-to-day relationships, springing naturally out of the situations and conversations we engage in. We should not artificially introduce our faith into every encounter, and any attempt to do so would again be doing the gospel a great disservice. Nor should every time we mention Christ involve overt evangelism – very few would put up with that for long! Rather, Christian commitment needs to be integrated into every part of life, so that it is reflected in the way we live and able to crop up in conversations in a way that is neither intrusive nor contrived. I do not believe there is a foolproof evangelistic method that can be applied to every situation, nor would I want to find one. No doubt the plethora of tools, programmes and other resources on the market today have their place, but we must beware of turning these into gimmicks or cure-alls, imagining that we need the latest product if we are to share our faith effectively. It is simply not so. There will never be a sub-stitute for ordinary people sharing naturally and spontaneously with those around them what Christ means in their lives. Lose that underlying truth and we will be in danger of losing everything.

In this course, I have highlighted six aspects of sharing our faith. First, we must be awake to the opportunities that God affords us, ready to grasp them when and where someone gives us a lead. Second, we must keep things simple, avoiding the temptation to become embroiled in theological debate, or to push any denomina-tional line. Third, our words must be reinforced by actions; what we do is more important than what we say. Fourth, we need to keep in mind those we are talking to, sensitive to their situation and ensuring we speak in terms they will understand. Fifth, there can be no substitute for speaking from the heart, for this is more important than all the evangelistic techniques and programmes put together. Finally, we must know when to stop, recognising that we can do more harm than good if we push the gospel upon those who do not want to hear it. We must never forget the vital truth underlying any form of mission or evangelism; namely, that results are ultimately dependent on God rather than ourselves.

This book offers no definitive blueprint for sharing our faith. I have as much to learn as anyone, being all too conscious of how rarely and inadequately I share my own faith outside of my writing ministry. In our modern-day world, where some ridicule the gospel and others simply consider it irrelevant, it is not easy to speak of Christ, particularly when we fear doing so might lead others to cari-cature our true position. Today, also, we need to be especially sensi-tive to those of other faiths, and to the potential tensions that might be caused through aggressive evangelism. Yet, having said that, we must never forget that we have been given good news in Christ, news that has fashioned our lives – in short, something to share.

Nick Fawcett

Leader's notes

I suggest using the material in this book as follows:

- Each session begins with a traditional prayer, followed by a short paragraph introducing the overall theme. It is worth reading this aloud, to set the scene for the session.

- After this I have included 'Activity' sessions, designed to break the ice and to encourage informal reflection on the theme of the study. Allow ten minutes or so for these, but do not allow them to dominate the session.

- Next comes a Bible passage (my own paraphrase unless otherwise stated). This should be read aloud, and then time given for group members to quietly ponder its meaning.

- Ideally, group members need to have read the 'Comment' section before the meeting, in which case you will need to have circulated booklets in advance of the first session. Alternatively, extend the period of quiet after the reading so that participants can read this section at their own pace.

- The 'Summary' section highlights the key points of the Comment. The leader should read this aloud before inviting people's thoughts on the subject so far.

- Allow discussion to develop and introduce as appropriate the questions provided in the Discussion section. It may be appropriate at this point to bring in the passage suggested for further reading, though you may prefer to leave this, as I have done, to round off the theme nearer the end.

- Pause for prayer, using the prayer provided, a prayer of your own, or a time of quiet / open prayer.

- After allowing ample time for discussion, read the meditation to draw people's thoughts together. The meditations in weeks 2 and 6 were written specially for this book; the others are taken from my earlier publications *No Ordinary Man* and *To Put It Another Way*.

- Briefly, outline the suggestions for action. Invite any further ideas from among the group. From the second week onwards, you might also give people the opportunity to share how they applied the suggestions from the previous week.
- Finally, end the meeting in prayer, using either the prayer provided or your own.

Prayer

Lord Jesus Christ,
    you call us to go out and proclaim the gospel,
    to make disciples of all nations,
    to demonstrate the reality of your love through word and deed.
We want to honour that calling,
    but we are aware of the danger
    of doing more harm than good through our witness,
    of putting people off rather than drawing them to faith.
So now we pray once more for your guidance in mission.
You have given us good news.
Teach us how to share it.

Inspire and enable us to speak for you when the opportunity arises,
    not to fail in our responsibilities
    or to rely on others to do what we should do ourselves,
    but to tell gladly and honestly what you mean to us
    and what you have done in our lives.
You have given us good news.
Teach us how to share it.

Show us those times when it is right to speak out,
    when the soil is ready to receive the seed of your word
    and bear harvest.
But teach us also when it is necessary to let go,
    to recognise that we have done our best and
    must leave things in your hands.
You have given us good news.
Teach us how to share it.

Save us from making excuses to evade the call to witness,
    but save us also from pushing people against their will,
    forcing our faith upon those for whom it is not welcome.

Teach us when it is time to speak and time to remain silent,
    time to encourage and time to hold back,
    time to try again and time to move on.
You have given us good news.
Teach us how to share it.

And teach us also that words are never enough;
    that it is the quality of our caring,
    the sincerity of our love
    and the genuineness of our actions
    which will finally speak the loudest.
Grant that, like you,
    what we say will be matched by what we do
    and what we believe show in who we are.
You have given us good news.
Teach us how to share it.

Lord Jesus Christ,
    you have touched our lives,
    you have brought us joy,
    you have given us life in all its fullness
    and we want to share with others the blessing we have received.
Inspire us through your love,
    equip us through your Spirit,
    and send us out to make you known.
You have given us good news.
Teach us how to share it.
In your name we pray.
Amen.

First week

No one told me

Opening prayer

Most merciful Father,
  I confess that I have done little
  to promote your kingdom
  and advance your glory.
Pardon my shortcomings
  and give me greater enthusiasm in serving you.
Make me more ready
  and conscientious by my prayers,
  my giving and my example,
  to spread the knowledge of your truth
  and extend your kingdom;
  and may I do everything to your glory.
Amen.
William Walsham How

Introduction

The note was clear enough: meet me at Linacre College at 3pm. It was sent by the don appointed to be my tutor during my time in Oxford, so on the day in question I consulted my map and set off early, determined to make the best possible beginning. I arrived with ample time to spare, or so at least I thought, only there was one problem – no college! With mounting consternation I retraced my steps, scrutinising the map to make sure I was in the right place, suppressing a rising tide of panic as the minutes ticked by on my watch. It was no good; the college simply wasn't there. I dived into a phone booth, rang the college number, and was greeted by an irate voice that became even more irritable as I explained my predicament. The college, it turned out, had moved several years previously; the map I was using was out of date by some time. When I eventually turned up, flustered and breathless, it was to a decidedly unhappy first meeting, my tutor proving to be someone who did not suffer fools gladly and clearly considering me a case in point! If only someone had told me that the college had moved, it might all have been so different, but, of course, everyone assumed I already knew.

You will, I'm sure, have grasped the analogy. We take it for granted, don't we, that all those we mix with have heard the gospel countless times before, and that there's therefore no need to repeat it, but is that really the case? Certainly, they may have a vague idea of what the Christian faith is about, derived perhaps from school assemblies, religious education lessons, and various portrayals in the media, but many have little more than the most sketchy knowledge of what the gospel has to say. As the Apostle Paul observed, 'How . . . can they call on one in whom they have not believed, and believe in one of whom they have never heard?' The answer, of course, is that they can't. Unless people are told about Jesus, they will never come to faith. At one time, those words were a rallying call to mission overseas; today they apply as much, if not more so, to the situation here at home. The temptation is to leave the telling to someone else; the danger is that no one else will tell them! We may not all be sent as missionaries or evangelists, but we all have a story to tell, a faith to proclaim. Isn't it time we shared it?

Activity

Embarrassing moments (see page 65).

Reading: Acts 8:30-31, 34-35

Running up to the chariot, Philip heard the [eunuch] reading Isaiah the prophet, so he asked him, 'Do you understand these words you're reading?' The eunuch answered, 'How can I possibly do that unless someone explains them to me?' And he urged Philip to come up and sit with him. The eunuch asked Philip, 'Tell me, who is the prophet talking about here? Does he refer to himself or someone else?' Then Philip, beginning with that passage of Scripture, talked to him about Jesus.

Comment

During my ministry, I seemed to hear one phrase more than any other: 'No one told me.' Those words echoed like the constantly repeated chorus of some modern worship songs, one person after another coming to me with the same complaint. Were we failing in our evangelistic responsibilities? Well, yes, we probably were, but that wasn't the problem here. It was simply the fact that people within the church were failing to communicate properly, too many pursuing their own agendas without any reference to others. A committee organised an event to take place on such and such a day, only to discover that another committee had organised their own event for the same date. 'No one told me!' came the outraged cry. Perhaps a church member was unwell or had cause for cel-ebration, but the grapevine had become snarled up so that only half the church came to hear about it. 'Why wasn't I kept informed? No one told me!' Perhaps someone had the temerity to rearrange the church office or undertake some duty without first seeking approval, and in the process metaphorically trod on someone's toes. 'Who said they could do that? No one told me!' Or perhaps a meeting had to be cancelled at short notice or its venue changed, but somehow the message didn't get round. 'What's going on? No one told me!'

To be fair, the problem of communication is one that bedevils not just the Church but almost every organisation you might care to mention. Wherever people get together, you have a recipe for discord and misunderstanding. It is a simple and inescapable fact that wires sometimes become crossed and communication breaks down. What *one* regards as vital news *another* considers a trivial snippet of information, and so fails to share it. What *I* may believe everyone has a right to know, *you* may feel, for reasons of discretion, shouldn't be publicised, and so once again it isn't passed on. More likely still, we simply forget to tell people what's happening, fully intending to do so only for it to slip our mind.

Another factor, however, probably exceeds all the others put together: the assumption that someone else will pass it on. 'It will get round,' we tell ourselves, 'no need for me to bother.' Imagine if Philip had said that when he spotted the Ethiopian eunuch travelling back to Gaza on the road from Jerusalem. Clearly here was a man searching for truth, thirsty for spiritual fulfilment, but was it up to Philip to respond to that need? He could well have argued that someone else was bound to tell him of Christ, or that it was only a matter of time before such eager searching of the scriptures brought its own enlightenment, but, of course, he didn't do either of those. For Philip, here was a God-given chance to make known the good news, and he grasped it with both hands. Perhaps the eunuch *would* have heard of Christ elsewhere, but Philip wasn't prepared to leave it to chance. As far as he was concerned, it was down to him. Jesus was relying on *him* to share his faith, and he wasn't going to waste the opportunity.

The result was an encounter that was to change the Ethiopian's life. One moment the prophet's words were a mystery, and the next they were wonderfully alive. One moment the eunuch was confused, the next he found enlightenment. One moment he was searching vainly for truth, and the next he was in no doubt he had found it.

It is surely no accident that the passage he was reading included the words 'How beautiful upon the mountains are the feet of the messenger who announces peace, who brings good news, who announces salvation' (Isaiah 52:7a, *NRSV*). Could such words be applied to us? Have we been the bringer of good news?

14

Have we passed on the gospel, making the most of the openings that come our way? Will anyone come to faith because we had the courage to speak of Christ?

We are those entrusted with good news, news that we are told to pass on, not by me or the Church but by Christ himself: 'You will receive power when the Holy Spirit has come upon you; and you will be my witnesses in Jerusalem, in all Judea and Samaria, and to the ends of the earth' (Acts 1:8, *NRSV*). All of us, no doubt, will pay lip service to that challenge, but do we ever act upon it? I'm not suggesting for a moment we should constantly be spouting religion or forever preaching the gospel – to do that would almost certainly hinder rather than further the cause of Christ – but when a golden opportunity presents itself, when we see someone hungry to find out more, are we ready to reach out and share our faith? Don't assume that someone else will do it. Don't promise to do your bit next time, when you're less busy, more confident, better equipped to meet the challenge. God asks you and me to tell the news, to share what Christ has done for us, and if we fail in that responsibility, one day we may the hear the words 'No one told me', and know to our shame that we are us much to blame as any.

Summary

- In churches, as in so many places and groups where people come together, communication can be a problem. For a variety of reasons, news and information are not passed on.
- A major reason is that we assume someone else will tell people, so we needn't bother. The result is that some people are missed out, never hearing the news at all.
- If Philip had assumed that someone else would tell the Ethiopian eunuch about Christ, he might never have come to faith. Philip saw that this man was searching for understanding, and recognised God was giving him an opportunity to share his faith and speak for Christ.

- Philip's testimony was instrumental in changing the eunuch's life. He turned out to be the right person in the right place at the right time.
- Like Philip, we too have good news to share. Jesus himself has called us to be his witnesses. Do we honour that calling, or will someone one day say about the gospel, 'No one told me', and point the finger accusingly at us?

Discussion

- Do you still see the gospel as good news? What would you say if someone asked you what Jesus means to you? Have there been times when you missed opportunities to communicate your faith?
- What things hold us back from talking of Christ? How far are these reasons justified? How can we overcome our reservations when we ought to speak out?
- Who was instrumental in leading us to faith? What did they say to us? What did we find most helpful? Were attempts made that we found unhelpful? What were these?

Prayer

Lord Jesus Christ,
    you call each of us,
    as you call all your people,
    to go out and proclaim the gospel.
Forgive us for failing to honour that calling;
    for being only too ready to come to you
    but less willing to go out in your name,
    eager to receive
    but reluctant to give.
Help us to recognise our responsibility towards others –

to understand that if we leave it to someone else
to share the good news of Christ
they may never hear it at all.
Fill us, then, with new vision and resolve,
so that when the opportunity comes to speak for you,
we may do so –
faithfully, honestly, sensitively and joyfully –
to the glory of your name.
Amen.

Meditation of Philip

I have to tell you!
Forgive me if I'm intruding,
barging in where I'm not wanted,
but I have to tell you what Christ has done for me.
I'm not bragging, God forbid!
There's been no merit on my part,
nothing about me that's special or deserving of praise.
I'm just an ordinary person,
no different from anyone else,
but I've suddenly discovered what really matters in life,
what really counts.
I thought I knew already –
well, we all do, don't we? –
a good job,
loving partner,
nice home,
children;
you know the sort of thing.
And don't think I'm knocking those,
for they can all be precious,
all offer their own fulfilment.
But when I heard about Jesus,
met him for myself,

suddenly I discovered there is something else,
something more important than any of those,
able to give a whole new perspective on them all
and to answer my deepest needs.
I was set free from myself –
   my guilt,
   my sin,
   my shame –
   not suddenly becoming perfect
   but finding forgiveness,
   a new beginning –
   a multitude of new beginnings.
I was set free from the endless quest for pleasure,
   from the gods of greed and lust,
   pride and envy;
   learning there is more to life than the thirst for gain
   or the pursuit of success.
I was set free from fear and worry,
   despair and sorrow,
   and even in my darkest days
   I'm certain now that joy will surely come.
And, above all, I've been freed from death,
   knowing, though this life shall end, that I shall rise again!
So now do you see why I have to tell,
   why I have to let you know?
I've found so much,
   such hope, peace and happiness
   and I can't just sit on that as though it's mine and mine alone.
I have to pass it on,
   share it out,
   let you find it too;
   so forgive me if I'm intruding,
   but if you've got a moment
   please, please,
   let me tell you!

Further reading: Romans 10:14-15

How can they cry out to someone they have not believed in? How can they believe in someone they have never heard of? And how can they hear of him unless someone proclaims it to them? And how can anyone proclaim unless they are sent?

Suggestions for action

Is there someone who hasn't heard the message of the gospel whom you could have told? If so, resolve to make the most of your next opportunity, and when it comes, take it.

Closing prayer

Living God,
  you have given us glad tidings,
  good news for all people.
Save us from keeping it to ourselves.
In the name of Christ.
Amen.

Second week
Keep it simple

Opening prayer

Take away from me, O God,
  all pride and vanity,
  all boasting and forwardness,
  and give me the true courage
  that shows itself by gentleness;
  the true wisdom
  that shows itself by simplicity;
  and the true power
  that shows itself by modesty.
Amen.

Charles Kingsley

Introduction

Italy 0, Republic of Ireland 1. The result sent a shockwave throughout the world of football, for this sort of result just wasn't meant to
happen: a midget in terms of international experience defeating
one of the giants of the game. Yet happen it did, and it was by no
means the first surprise of its kind. Four years earlier, in the 1990
World Cup, the team from Eire had gone one better, not only qualify-
ing for the World Cup but making it all the way to the quarter-finals
before finally succumbing to the much-fancied Dutch. For a glorious
few years, a side sent their country wild with football fever, eclipsing
rugby union and Gaelic sports as the traditional national game – a
truly astonishing achievement.

So what was the secret of their success? What shrewd strategy
and cutting-edge tactics lay behind this unexpected transformation

of fortunes? The answer is very simple: none! Or, to be more accurate, none that was anything new. The philosophy of Jack Charlton, the team's manager at the time, was to keep things simple, to play the game by the most direct route by getting the ball as often as possible into the opponent's penalty area. Purists may have torn out their hair in disgust and disbelief, but the fans loved it, thrills and spills almost guaranteed.

The message is clear enough: simplicity worked. The players not only understood what was expected of them but were also able to do it, and the results more than vindicated the method. We can apply that principle equally well to sharing our faith. Here, too, we do well to keep things uncomplicated, getting across our message as directly as possible rather than being drawn into the intricacies of theology and doctrine. Faith may not always be a straightforward matter but the gospel is, and we complicate it at our peril. Sometimes, the more we try to elaborate, the less people understand. Far better to point simply to Christ as best we can, and leave the rest to him.

Activity

News headlines (see page 65).

Reading: 1 Corinthians 1:17-24

Christ did not send me to baptise but to declare the gospel; not using clever words and concepts, in case those should empty the cross of Christ of its power. For the word of the cross to those who are perishing is folly, but to us who are being saved it is the power of God. For it is written, 'I will demolish the cleverness of the wise, and put a stop to the sharpness of the shrewd.' Where is the wise person? Where the scribe? Where are the philosophers of this age? Has not God made worldly wisdom appear silly? For since, by his wisdom, the world could not fathom him through human intelligence, God decided, through the folly of our message, to save those who believe. Jews insist on signs and Greeks crave wisdom, but we proclaim Christ crucified, an offence to the Jews and plain folly to others, but to those who have been called, whether Jews or Greeks, it is the message of Christ, the power and wisdom of God.

Comment

This was astonishing, I thought. At last, an item of self-assembly furniture that truly was as easy to put together as the manufacturers claimed. Just the doors to put on and a shelf to fit and it would be finished, job done. Only what was this? The doors seemed to be back-to-front. Strange! And how could the shelf possibly fit into so tight a space? Stranger still! 'Why can't they get things right?' I muttered. 'Why is nothing ever made as it should be?' I looked again at the instructions, and slowly it dawned on me: that funny little drawing I'd puzzled over – the one that looks like a spaceship – and the arrow that appeared to point nowhere in particular – it meant that the hinges should be this side, not that, and that the shelf needed to be installed at the beginning, not the end. With that all-too-familiar sinking feeling that for me has become synonymous with flat-pack furniture, I realised that I would have to disassemble everything I had so painstakingly put together and start again from scratch.

Am I the only one who invariably ends up in the throes of despair when undertaking such projects? I may be, for DIY was never my forte, but I suspect I am not alone. Manufacturers may believe they have simplified their instructions to the point that even a two-year-old can understand them, and the carpenters of this world may refer to MFI furniture as 'made for idiots', but what seems crystal clear to one may be baffling to others. The same can be true when it comes to sharing our faith. Without realising it, we may as well sometimes be talking another language for all the success we have in getting our message across. I'm not talking here about the jargon we can sometimes slip into; we will deal with that in a later session. I'm talking rather about the danger of complicating the gospel, feeling perhaps that we must spell out every detail of doctrine, explain the mysteries of the creed, prove the virgin birth, or defend the inspiration of Scripture. All too easily we can find ourselves drawn into argument, seeking to justify the Church or excuse the faults of individual Christians. Equally, we may fall into the trap of pushing a party line, promoting the things we believe as Anglicans, Catholics, Baptists or whatever, rather than communicating the simple message of the gospel. Instead of sharing, we end up squabbling.

'Very true,' I hear you say, 'only, of course, that could never apply to me. I tell the gospel as it is: nothing added, nothing taken away – the essential indisputable bare bones of faith.' Don't you believe it! You may fondly imagine that you are different, but the fact is that we all have our own perception of faith and our own emphases within that – perhaps inherited from our parents, family and friends; perhaps learned within our fellowship or denomination; or perhaps picked up in devotional reading, Christian conferences or religious broadcasting. That is not to say this is wrong – far from it. We all need to make sense of the gospel, to work through its implications and so make it ours in the sense that it touches our lives, but having done that, when it comes to talking to others about Christ, we need to get back to basics, to the essentials rather than the niceties of faith.

This is precisely what we see in Paul's words to the Corinthians, his message summarised in one phrase: 'Christ crucified . . . the power and wisdom of God.' It may not have seemed much in comparison to the great oratory of his day, and the Jews may have condemned it as blasphemy – he didn't care. Here, for Paul, was the gospel in miniature, so simple yet so profound! Yes, of course it needed fleshing out – in his letters, Paul added more flesh than most! – but the more we add to it, the more we risk complicating and losing the vital truth at its heart. As Paul expressed it, we are called simply 'to declare the gospel; not using clever words and concepts, in case those should empty the cross of Christ of its power'

(1 Corinthians 1:17). Most of us, I suspect, would want to expand Paul's summary to 'Christ crucified and risen'. Others would want to add still more, but if that's you, then, before you do, stop and ask yourself why. Is it the *gospel* you're concerned to safeguard or your interpretation of it? There's a difference between the two.

Remember that, the next time you talk about or attempt to share your faith. Don't get sidetracked into blind alleys. Don't dwell on peripherals, however important they may be to you. Above all, don't bombard people with doctrine or jargon, attempting to make them a Baptist or Anglican, charismatic or traditionalist, liberal or fundamentalist. Keep things simple, and leave the rest to God.

Summary

- What may seem a clear straightforward message to one may seem anything but to another. All too easily, we make things more complicated than they need to be.

- As Christians, we can be sidetracked into peripheral issues, or into arguments that alienate people from Christ rather than make them want to find out more. Instead of sharing the bare bones of the gospel, we can become embroiled in issues of doctrine, denominational emphasis or personal conviction.

- We may imagine that *we* are different, but we all have a unique experience of faith and all put our own interpretations upon that. It is difficult to present the simple challenge of Christ rather than what we consider that simple challenge to be.

- Paul summarised the message of the gospel as 'Christ crucified'. We will want to enlarge on that to 'Christ crucified and risen', as Paul would surely have done too if asked for a formal summary, but we need to beware of adding too many extras. We may believe that much is important but we need to focus on what is essential.

- We are not called to win people over to our church or Christian tradition, but simply to proclaim Christ. We can leave the rest in God's hands.

Discussion

- How would you sum up the essential ingredients of the gospel? In what ways do you feel its message has been overcomplicated?
- Why have various creeds and statements of faith developed over the years? What is the value of these? What are the dangers?
- How hard is it to keep faith simple? Have there been times when you have been drawn out of your depth? Can the message be too simple?

Prayer

Gracious God,
    we thank you for the simplicity of the gospel –
    the message of your great love shown in Christ.
We thank you that it is not about clever words or subtle concepts,
    but about the concrete expression of your love.
Forgive us for complicating that message –
    for cluttering it up with our ideas and prejudices,
    our attempts to define and delimit,
    our interpretations and terminology.
Open our eyes again to all you have done for us,
    and help us to communicate the simple message
    of Christ crucified and risen.
In his name we ask it.
Amen.

Meditation of Paul

I wasn't much of a preacher,
    not compared to my peers, anyway.
In terms of style,
    technique,
    rhetoric,

they were in a different league,
a class of their own,
and they weren't backward in telling me, either!
Did it hurt?
It might have done, but for one thing:
people listened,
and responded,
more to me than to them!
Oh yes, they were masters of their craft all right,
gifted orators such as I could never hope to be,
but they wove words for their own sake,
ultimately constructing a web so complex
they became lost within it,
ensnared by their own artifice,
offering more questions than answers,
more heat than light.
That wasn't for me.
I knew my limitations
and thankfully they didn't matter,
for God had given me one thing to proclaim,
one message to share:
Christ crucified and risen.
Not much, you say?
Don't you believe it,
for there we see the power and wisdom of God –
so awesome
yet so simple.
It's not about us –
what *we* think,
what *we* say –
but about *him* –
what *God* has done,
what *he* is doing.
He came,
he died,
he rose again in Christ –

the greatest of gifts,
the most inexpressible love –
what more could we need to add?
It changed my life,
it's changed others,
and so long as people continue to share that gospel,
as I have done,
it will go on changing lives to the end of time,
for it's not the speaker that matters
but the message –
the simple message that says it all.

Further reading: John 3:16

God loved the world so much that he offered his only Son, so that all those who believe in him will not die but have everlasting life.

Suggestions for action

Write down in one short sentence the essence of the gospel, as you understand it. Assess during the coming week how far you live by that summary and in what ways you succeed in communicating it.

Closing prayer

Living God,
for the simple yet wonderful message
that in Christ you lived and died among us,
and that in him you defeated death,
rising again so that we might live,
we thank you,
in his name.
Amen.

Third week

Practising what we preach

Opening prayer

Stay with me, Lord Jesus,
  so that I shall begin to shine as you shine,
  as a light to others.
The light will be all from you.
It will be you who shine through me upon others.
Give light to them as well as to me;
  light them with me, through me.
Help me witness to you without preaching;
  not by words but by example
  and by the sympathetic influence of what I do;
  by my visible resemblance to your saints
  and the evident fullness of my love for you.
Amen.

John Henry Newman

Introduction

What would you say is the accusation most commonly levelled by non-Christians against the Church? In my experience, one far out-weighs all the others: the charge of hypocrisy. In part, this probably simply reflects misunderstanding as to what Christians actually believe – a feeling still rife, though generally misplaced, that we regard ourselves as better than others (if anything, we should believe the opposite). In part, also, the accusation is used by some as a useful stick with which to beat the Church, condemnation providing an easy way out of facing the challenge of the gospel. Sadly, however, there is sufficient truth in the charge to give it some credence in the eyes of many. We talk of love, yet all too often fail to show it; of unity, yet are manifestly divided; of forgiveness, yet are judgemental in our attitudes – and so it goes on. Admittedly, we might protest that none of us claims to be perfect, yet this does not diminish the impact of our failure to live up to the faith we proclaim. People will judge us, and ultimately Christ too, not by what we say but by what we do, on whether our words are matched by deeds, our preaching backed up by practice.

Activity

Fishing game (see page 66).

Reading: Matthew 5:14-16

You are the light of the world. Just as a city situated on a mountain-top cannot be hidden, so nobody lights a lamp and places it under a bushel basket, putting it instead on a lamp-stand in order that it might shed light throughout the house. Similarly, let the light in you shine before others, so that they may see the good deeds you do and give glory to your heavenly Father.

Comment

In my garden, I recently planted a new shrub, the well-known buddleia or 'butterfly bush'. The nickname is well chosen, for there is something about buddleia that attracts butterflies and bees in their droves. Quite simply, they find its scent irresistible, in much the same way as a moth is drawn to light, or iron by a magnet. It would be nice to suggest that the Church might exert a similar attraction, but I doubt even the most zealous of Christians seriously expects that. Typically, the world passes it by with sublime indifference, not particularly hostile but neither particularly interested, and that's probably the way things will always be. Yet if we do not expect people to come flocking to our doors like bees around a honey pot, this does not mean that we can simply put it down to general apathy; we need to take a long hard look at ourselves, as individuals and as fellowships of believers, and ask ourselves whether all is as it should be. Whatever else, there should be something about us that sets us apart; a quality of love, integrity, commitment, compassion – call it what you will – that causes people to pause and reflect.

It is with this in mind that we need to read those words of Jesus in the Sermon on the Mount: 'Let the light in you shine before others, so that they may see the good deeds you do and give glory to your heavenly Father' (Matthew 5:16). We cannot simply talk about light – we must shed it. That is a truth fundamental to any talk of mission or evangelism. Christians need to be seen as well as heard! Our lives should speak to others of Christ without the need for words, faith displaying itself in action. Instead of simply speaking about love, we must show it to others. Instead of talking about forgiveness, we need to show it in our relationships. Yes, words have their place, for without them we could not communicate very much, and, yes, there are times when we need to speak out for the gospel, publicly to declare our faith in Christ. Ultimately, though, talking about faith is the easy part; the hard part is translating it into daily life. We may have the most sophisticated outreach programme in the world and be the most gifted of evangelists. It doesn't matter – if our preaching isn't backed up by practice, few will want to listen. Would the crowds have followed Jesus in such numbers if he'd said one thing and done another? Of course not! What set him apart and made his message irresistible is that words and deeds were one, what he preached underpinned by what he did, and what he did illuminating what he said. That's why the crowds thronged about him and hung on to his every word: because who he was measured up to what he claimed to be.

We in turn are called to a similar quality and transparency of life. Not that we will attain it, but this is the vision we reach for, the target towards which we aspire. It is the goal spelled out by Jesus in his great prayer for the unity of the Church: 'As you, Father, are in me and I am in you, may they also be in us, so that the world may believe that you have sent me. The glory that you have given me, I have given them, so that they may be one, as we are one, I in them and you in me, that they may become completely one, so that the world may know that you have sent me and have loved them even as you have loved me' (John 17:21-23, *NRSV*). We are not simply talking about the unity of the Church here, nor of the Father with Son. We are talking also of the unity between word and deed, of lives that reflect the God we claim to serve in Christ. If we would witness to our faith, communicating with others the truth of the gospel, then there is no better way of doing that than through the way we live and the people we are. Here is where all mission ultimately stands or falls.

What, then, do people see when they look at you and me? We aren't perfect, we know that, and neither will anyone but the most critical expect us to be, but is there enough in the way we live for people to take our faith seriously? As some have put it, if we were put on trial for our faith, would there be enough evidence to convict us, or would we find ourselves charged with fraud, accused along with the Church in general of hypocrisy? It's an important question for, like it or not, we're on trial every day, somebody somewhere measuring the faith we proclaim by the way we live it.

The question is important for another reason too. The butterfly bush does not just attract bees and butterflies by an accident of nature; it does so for a purpose, relying on them to spread pollen and so ensure new plants for the future! If it fails to attract them, then it fails to secure a new generation, and if every bush suffered the same problem, then the species would soon die out. So it is also with the Church: its future in large part depends on our faithfulness to the call of Christ. As Christians we have something to share, but we will never get it across if our words say one thing and our lives another. Are we practising what we preach?

31

Summary

- Just as butterflies and bees are attracted by a butterfly bush, so there should be something about our lives and the Church that attracts people. If we are met only with indifference, we need to ask ourselves if everything is as it should be.

- Jesus calls us to let our light shine before others. His words remind us that talk is not enough; faith needs to be translated into action. The secret of his own ministry is that his deeds were consistent with his words.

- Our goal should be to live in similar fashion. The quality of our life will ultimately speak more powerfully than anything we may say.

- Do our lives back up our words? Would people know that we are Christians without us having to tell them? Could anyone charge us with hypocrisy?

- If we fail to attract people, then the Church will soon cease to exist. Are we practising what we preach?

Discussion

- 'Actions speak louder than words.' How far do you think that is true? Can you think of examples from your own experience that reinforce the point?

- Whose lives have spoken most powerfully to you of the love of Christ?

- In what ways do you bring light to others? How far does your life proclaim Christ and how far does it deny him?

- What do you find hardest about turning faith into action? Which aspects of practical discipleship do you find most daunting?

Prayer

Lord Jesus Christ,
   forgive us that so often our lives betray our calling
   and deny your love.
Forgive us when people look at us
   and instead of seeing something of you, see only ourselves.
Forgive us when the things we say and do obscure the gospel,
   rather than proclaim its message to all.
Help us truly to reflect your love,
   show your compassion
   and shed your light to others.
Renew and restore us by your grace.
   so that we may shine like stars in the world,
   bringing glory to you and your Father in heaven,
   for your name's sake.
Amen.

Meditation of a listener to the Sermon on the Mount

Had he made a mistake?
I thought he must have, at first.
'*You* are the light of the world' –
   it had to be wrong, surely?
That was *him* wasn't it, not *us* –
   he the one who brings light to those walking in darkness?
At least that's what I'd always believed,
   that one day God would send a Messiah
   whose glory would shine like a beacon in the world,
   all nations drawn by his radiance
   and nothing able to overshadow the brightness of his coming.
So what was *this* all about,
   turning the tables on us
   so that suddenly *we* were the ones called to be light,
   we those with the responsibility of scattering the darkness?

It was the last thing I expected,
and the last thing I'd bargained on,
for I knew that on my own I could scarcely raise a flicker,
let alone a light bright enough to bring glory to God.
If it was down to *my* efforts,
my faith,
then there'd be no hope for anyone, would there?
And, of course, *he* knew that, as much as anyone.
It's *his* grace that floods our souls,
his love that fills our hearts,
his light that shines in our lives,
and without that we can do nothing.
But that doesn't mean we can simply sit back
and leave it all to him,
for, alongside what he has done for *us*,
faith is about what we can do for *him*!
It involves giving as well as receiving,
serving as well as being served,
and we need to do that not simply when the mood takes us,
but every day, every moment,
the call at the very heart of discipleship –
the essence of faith.
The light of the world –
yes, it means *you* as well as him,
for though ultimately *he* is the true light,
the one who illuminates the way for all,
he needs *your* love,
your deeds,
your compassion,
your faith translated into action
if the darkness is not to close in and his light be obscured.
'Let your light shine before others,
so that they may see your good works
and give glory to your Father in heaven.'
He said it,
and he meant it!

Further reading: Philippians 2:14-16a

Do everything without arguing or complaint, so that you may be irreproachable beyond causing offence, above criticism in a decadent and corrupt generation, shining like stars in the world and thus holding up the word of life to all.

Suggestions for action

Do something practical this week that expresses your faith in action.

Closing prayer

Living God,
   as the dew falls in the morning,
   so may your grace descend upon us,
   and as the sun bathes all in its life-giving light,
   so may the radiance of Christ shine in our hearts.
Work in us,
   with us,
   and through us
   to your glory.
Amen.

Fourth week

Speaking their language

Opening prayer

Lord, make me a messenger
  of your love.
To the searching heart
  send me with your word;
  to the aching heart
  send me with your peace;
  to the broken heart
  send me with your love.
However small or wide my world, Lord,
  let me warm it with the promise
  that you care.
Amen.

Author unknown

Introduction

If someone were to regale you with Einstein's theory of relativity, how long would it be before you excused yourself? Unless you happened to be a physicist, I expect you would look for the earliest opportunity. The subject may be fascinating to experts, but to most of us it is virtually another language. Communication is about speaking to people in terms they can relate to.

This perhaps accounts for the astonishing success of the Apostle Paul throughout his ministry. Look at the way he addressed the people of Athens. As a Jew, his inclination must have been to talk of Jesus in terms of Old Testament prophecy, and, as a Pharisee, in terms of the Jewish law; but he did neither, because he knew such concepts would mean nothing to his Greek listeners. He needed to speak to them in terms of their own faith and culture, and that is precisely what he did, quoting, in a masterstroke, from Epimenides and Aratus, two of their own poets – in other words, talking their language. Do we do that when we share our faith, or do we talk over people's heads? Do we attempt to relate what we are saying to daily life or simply repeat doctrine and religious jargon parrot-fashion? Effective testimony takes two things: a willingness to speak honestly about what God means to us, and a sensitivity towards those we are talking to, so that God may speak in turn to them.

Activity

Cracking the code (see page 66).

Reading: Acts 17:22-28

Standing in the middle of the Areopagus, Paul said, 'People of Athens, I perceive that you are deeply religious, for as I walked by I couldn't help noticing your objects of worship, among which I spotted an altar on which was inscribed "To an unknown god". What you worship as unknown, I now proclaim to you. The God who created the world and all things in it, the Lord of heaven and earth, does not live in shrines made by human hands, nor is he served in the sense of being dependent on anyone. Rather, he gives breath and life to all things. He created all nations that live on earth from a common ancestor, and he established the times and limits of their existence so that they will search for God and, should they grope after him, eventually find him – although ultimately he is not far from any of us. In him we live, move and have our being, as indeed some of your own poets have said, "For we also are his offspring".'

Comment

As a proofreader and copy-editor, I get to read many words, and when I say many I mean it! Last year alone, I read over 40 text-books from cover to cover, each averaging around 400 pages. I like to imagine there are few words I haven't come across, but I'm repeatedly made to think again. Many is the time I've been tempted to cross something through, certain it's a mistake, only to check in the dictionary and find it's a word after all. The worlds of economics, archaeology, special-needs education and ecology each have a language of their own. To the outsider, it might as well be double-Dutch, but to those in the know its meaning is clear as day.

So it is too with religion; an important lesson that can never be learned too thoroughly! To the Christian or regular churchgoer – that is, the insider – the language of the Bible or the Church means, or at least should mean, a great deal. So, for example, we speak of fellowship, the Holy Spirit, eternal life, or of being 'saved', 'born again', and the 'body of Christ'. We know what we mean by such terms, but to the person in the street they can seem as strange and unintelligible as the most complicated technical terms or some obscure foreign language. Such language doesn't touch them where they are, failing to ring any bells in their everyday experience, and as a result they dismiss it as irrelevant, for others rather than for them.

Perhaps here we see one of the reasons why Jesus chose the people he did to be his disciples. Contrary to what one might have expected, he didn't choose scribes or Pharisees, priests of rabbis – those who were acknowledged experts in religion. He didn't pick people known for their learning or intellectual ability, their skill in public speaking or proven ability with words. Instead, he called down-to-earth people, or, as Acts 4:13 puts it,'unschooled, ordinary men', and because they were just that, they were able to get along-side people, speak to them in a language they understood and meet them where they were. At times, they were sharing things that they didn't fully understand themselves, trying to put into words truths that finally defied expression, but, if nothing else, they tried to make sense of these by putting them into their own words.

We see much the same thing in the ministry of Jesus himself. His favourite way of teaching the crowds was to make use of parables. He didn't harangue them with long and complicated expositions of Scripture; he didn't deliver erudite lectures; he didn't even preach three-point sermons! Instead he told them stories: stories about people, places and objects they could relate to – a lost sheep, lost coin, lost son; an unjust manager, faithful steward, persistent widow; a vine, fig tree, mustard seed; salt, light, yeast. Here were terms that his listeners could relate to. They might not agree with everything he said or understand its full import, but, having listened to him, no one would have gone back home scratching their head and muttering, 'What was he on about?'

So it was also with the Apostle Paul as he preached to the people of Athens. As we noted in our second session, he made no claim to be the best preacher in the world, but as far as possible he attempted to get alongside those he was speaking to. Having been schooled as a Pharisee, his natural inclination must have been to talk about Christ in terms of Judaism, as indeed he often did in his letters, when writing to those of a Jewish background or where observance of the Jewish law had become an issue. He could have talked about Jesus as the Messiah, about the way, through his coming, he fulfilled Old Testament prophecy, and about his sacrifice as a paschal lamb, but what would that have meant to the Athenians? Nothing! For them, the Old Testament was a closed book and Judaism just one obscure religion among many. So he spoke instead about their beliefs and culture, pointing to an altar in their own city. In other words, he met them on their home ground, explaining what Christ could mean to them. 'People of Athens, I perceive that you are deeply religious, for as I walked by I couldn't help noticing your objects of worship, among which I spotted an altar on which was inscribed "To an unknown god". What you worship as unknown, I now proclaim to you' (Acts 17:22-23). Then, in a masterstroke, he quoted from Epimenides and Aratus, two respected Greek philosophers (or poets, as he calls them): 'He is not far from any of us. In him we live, move and have our being, as indeed some of your own poets have said, "For we also are his offspring"' (Acts 17: 27b-28). Paul uses every means at his disposal to ensure that his words make contact with his listeners, and it is clear from what he tells us elsewhere that this was by no means an isolated instance. 'I have made myself a slave to all, so that I might win more of them. To the Jews I became as a Jew, in order to win Jews . . . to those outside the law I became as one outside the law . . . so that I might win those outside the law. To the weak I became weak, so that I might win the weak' (1 Corinthians 9:19b-22a, *NRSV*). This is not to say that Paul put on an act depending on which way the wind was blowing, or that he in any way altered or watered down the message of the gospel; simply that whenever and wherever he shared his faith, he stopped to consider first the people he was talking to.

Here is the key to any effective and meaningful sharing: speaking *to* people rather than *at* them! We are not only talking about avoiding the use of jargon, important though that is. We are talking also about sensitivity to the situations of those we are speaking to, striving, as far as possible, to put ourselves in their shoes and relate to them in a way that they can understand and that is appropriate to their circumstances. We are all different, and what one person needs to hear may not be the same as another. Similarly, what to some people seems straightforward will go over the heads of others, and what corresponds to the experience of some groups will be totally alien to those who move in different circles. The faith we proclaim may be the same but the way we present it may need to be very different, according to whom we are talking to. It's no good simply speaking of Christ and expecting everyone to listen; we must learn to tell others of what he means to *us* in language that means something to *them*! Only then will we be talking their language.

Summary

- Most disciplines employ their own technical language that is often incomprehensible to the outsider. The same is true when it comes to religion. As Christians we tend to use many terms that mean something to us but nothing to the average person. Because of this, Christianity is frequently dismissed as irrelevant.

- The Apostle Paul could easily have slipped into the jargon of Judaism when addressing the Athenians. Schooled as a Pharisee, Jewish terms and concepts would have come naturally to him. However, he resisted the temptation, knowing that it would fail to ring any bells among his listeners. Instead, he spoke in terms of their own faith, even borrowing words from their own poets.

- Instead of talking *at* people, he spoke *to* them, doing his best to get alongside them.

- This was clearly characteristic of Paul's general approach; he was willing to become all things to all people in order to win them for Christ.

- If we hope to communicate our faith, we have to emulate Paul, not just, as far as possible, avoiding religious language but also speaking in terms and concepts that our listeners can relate to.

Discussion

- Are there occasions when you have felt people are talking *at* you rather than *to* you? What were these? What specifically was the problem?

- How far is it possible to get alongside somebody from a different cultural situation to our own? Can we avoid being patronising on the one hand, or out of our depth on the other?

- What glaring examples of Christian jargon have you come across? Are there terms which you yourself don't understand?

41

Prayer

Lord of all,
    you call us to witness to Christ –
    to share with others what he has done in our lives.
Help us to do that wisely,
    sensitively,
    honestly
    and faithfully.
Teach us to speak from personal experience
    rather than by empty rote;
    to present the simple message of the gospel
    rather than the intricacies of doctrine or dogma;
    and, above all, to be conscious of those we are talking to
    instead of conscious of ourselves.
Whenever and wherever the opportunity presents itself,
    teach us to witness in a way that is relevant and alive,
    and so may your love be made known to all,
    in the name of Christ.
Amen.

Meditation of Dionysius the Areopagite

He spoke with conviction, that man – I'll give him that –
    as though he totally believed what he was saying.
The arguments may have been weak sometimes,
    not the same sophistication, the same subtlety,
    as from our own philosophers,
    and as an orator, to put it bluntly, I've heard better.
But he tried,
    he really tried to get his message home,
    more than anyone else I've ever met.
He'd done his homework too, that was clear,
    speaking to us on our own ground
    in terms we would understand,

language we could immediately relate to.
And he wasn't just playing games,
  out to prove some academic point or make his mark as a speaker.
You could see he was sincere,
  desperate to get his message home.
One rarely hears that here, you know,
  here, where ideas are two a penny
  and schools of thought vie together like brawling children,
  each resolved to win the day.
I've sat and listened many times
  while good and evil,
  life and death,
  are toyed with in debate like a toddler's plaything –
  diverting,
  rewarding for a time,
  but then casually put aside until another day.
Not Paul though –
  he talked as one who had to speak,
  of things that burned within him,
  and when he spoke of Jesus,
  it was with eyes aflame and face aglow.
I won't say I'm convinced,
  not yet at least;
  I'll have to hear him further before I go that far.
But I'm intrigued,
  eager to find out more,
  for when he spoke of death and then of life,
  of Jesus rising from the tomb,
  he talked as one who knew,
  as one who'd seen,
  as one who had no doubts.
Well, if he's right and Jesus really is alive,
  if he spoke truth and this man really rose,
  then I want to meet him, see him for myself;
  not put my trust in another's faith
  but root it in my own.

Can it be true?
It seems impossible,
   too good for words.
Yet there's no denying it, despite what his critics may say –
   he spoke with conviction, that man,
   with a passion I have rarely heard,
   and a passion I would love to share.

Further reading: 1 Corinthians 9:22b-23

I have become all things to all people, so that I might exploit every possibility to save them. Everything I do is for the sake of the gospel, so that I too may share in its blessings.

Suggestions for action

Write out your personal testimony and then go through it, picking out examples of jargon you have slipped into. Better still, talk to someone among your friends or family who is not a Christian, and ask them to identify terms and concepts that make no sense to them. Attempt to rephrase such jargon in your own words.

Closing prayer

Lord,
   you have given us good news to share.
Help us to remember not just the message
   but the people you want us to share it with,
   and so may we speak the words you would have us say
   in the way you would have us say them.
Amen.

Fifth week

_____ Words from the heart _____

Opening prayer

Grant, O Lord,
> that none may love you less this day
> because of me;
> that no word or act of mine
> may turn one soul from you;
> and for one more grace I dare to pray,
> that many people may love you more this day
> because of me.

Amen.

Eric Milner-White

Introduction

When I was a boy, an old pump stood outside my local park that had once been the main source of water for people living in the vicinity. All that, though, had been a long time ago, even back then in the 1960s. The workings had rusted away and the pumping lever was hopelessly jammed; in short, the pump had effectively run dry.

Many of us fear something similar to that might happen if ever we attempt to share our faith. It's not that we haven't anything to say – quite the contrary – but we inwardly dread starting to speak and then finding the words just won't come, our minds going blank at the vital moment. Witnessing for Christ, we tell ourselves, needs specialist knowledge, natural talent or unique gifts. Much though we'd like to have a go, it's a job best left to evangelists, clergy and missionaries, those who have been equipped for the task and acquired the necessary skills. Are we right? Emphatically and unequivocally not! Certainly those who are trained in public speaking, theology and the like may have advantages in certain situations, but that does not mean they alone are able to communicate the gospel effectively. Indeed, I have sat through sufficient dull sermons, and probably delivered a fair few of my own, to know that 'training' does not necessarily count for anything.

If anyone recognised that, it was Jesus. Consider those he called as Apostles. Were they scribes, Pharisees, the teachers of the law? No. Were they priests or rabbis, the religious specialists of his age? No. Instead, they were an unlikely ragbag, their ranks including a tax collector, freedom fighter, and fishermen. In other words, they were remarkably ordinary people who almost certainly hadn't the least experience of preaching or teaching between them, and I've no doubt their hearts must have sunk when Jesus suddenly sent them out into the mission field. What could they possibly hope to achieve? What conceivable impact could they make? It must have seemed ridiculous. Yet to each one Jesus gave the assurance that the Holy Spirit would give them the words they needed, when they needed them: 'When they hand you over, do not worry about how you are to speak or what you are to say; for what you are to say will be given to you at that time; for it is not you who speak, but the Spirit of your Father speaking through you' (Matthew 10:19).

What does that mean? The answer, of course, is many things, and no doubt scholars will continue to debate long and hard over the nature, experience and workings of the Holy Spirit, but in purely practical terms it surely means above all else speaking of what is in our heart. We may not be theologically precise or technically erudite, but that doesn't matter, for the sincerity of our faith will shine through and say more than words alone can ever do. Don't let the fear of running dry put you off. Don't assume there is some special qualification you need to share your faith with others. Tell, simply and sincerely, of what Christ means to you. The results may amaze you.

Activity

Immortal lines (see page 67).

Reading: Acts 4:1-3, 13, 18-21

While Peter and John were speaking to the people, the priests, the captain of the temple, and the Sadducees came to them, much annoyed because they were teaching the people and proclaiming that in Jesus there is the resurrection of the dead. So they arrested them and put them in custody until the next day, for it was already evening. Now when they saw the boldness of Peter and John and realised that they were uneducated and ordinary men, they were amazed and recognised them as companions of Jesus. They called them and ordered them not to speak or teach at all in the name of Jesus. But Peter and John answered them, 'Whether it is right in God's eyes to listen to you rather than to God, you must judge; for we cannot keep from speaking about what we have seen and heard.' After threatening them again, they let them go, finding no way to punish them because of the people, for all of them praised God for what had happened. (*NRSV*)

Comment

A few years ago a fascinating television documentary series asked the question 'What makes a great speaker?' Using archive film of such legends as Lloyd George, Winston Churchill, Martin Luther King, Billy Graham and Donald Soper, it highlighted some of the qualities needed to become a great orator. These included posture, gestures and mannerisms, power and inflection of voice, well-chosen pauses, eye contact, tempo, repetition and humour. I watched those programmes eagerly, hoping that next time I delivered a sermon the congregation would leap to their feet in wild and spontaneous applause, and that before long crowds would be flocking to my church in their droves! Sadly, it never happened and, of course, I never seriously imagined that it would, for truly gifted speakers are a rare breed. Yet there is more to effective communication than technique, learned or otherwise, and so it was for the orators above. As much as anything, the impact they made derived from the sincerity of their words, the fact that they spoke from the heart of things they deeply and passionately believed in. Without that, their words may still have sounded impressive, assuming they could still have been spoken, but they would have lacked their cutting edge.

If this was true for them, it must have been all the more so for the Apostles in the days of the early Church. Suddenly, here they were, entrusted with taking the gospel out into the world. It must have seemed daunting enough sharing it in Jerusalem and Judea, let alone in Samaria and to the ends of the earth, yet this was the challenge they faced. Where could they even begin? The answer, of course, was that alone they couldn't. They depended on the power of God's Spirit at work within them, but in what way did that Spirit move? Above all, surely, it was through the sincerity of their witness, the passionate enthusiasm of their words, the self-evident conviction oozing from every pore. Nowhere do we see that more clearly than in the example of Peter and John as they preached the gospel in Jerusalem following the coming of the Spirit at Pentecost. They knew the risks they were taking in speaking out, and soon found out how real these were as they found themselves hauled up before the chief priests and elders to explain their temerity in continuing to speak of Jesus. Yet, despite the threats made against them, they simply could not keep quiet. 'Peter and John answered them, "Whether it is right in God's sight to listen to you rather than to God, you must judge; for we cannot keep from speaking about what we have seen and heard"' (Acts 4:19-20, NRSV).

Fair enough, you may say, but perhaps these represent the exception that proves the rule. After all, their success was as nothing compared to that of the Apostle Paul, and if *they* weren't theologically trained, *he* was. Yet, true though that may be, Paul openly admitted to not being a patch on other speakers of his time, compared to whom, technically speaking, he came a very poor second. Furthermore, Paul clearly found the business of sharing his faith a frightening ordeal at times. As he wrote in his first letter to the Corinthians, 'I came to you in weakness and in fear, and in much trembling' (2:3 NRSV). Yet share he did, wherever and whenever he could, with astonishing success. In part, as we saw in our session last week, this was down to his willingness to talk the language of his listeners, but alongside that, I suspect, was his transparent sincerity. There was no artifice about Paul, none of what, in modern politics, we have come to refer to as 'spin'. He spoke of the way Jesus had changed his life, of the grace that constantly amazed him, of the love that moved him afresh each day, of the inner presence of the Holy Spirit that encouraged, nurtured, sustained and inspired him whatever he might face. Whatever Paul said or wrote, it came straight from the heart, and people responded accordingly.

When it comes to communication, the impact of sincerity cannot be emphasised too strongly. We may be the most polished speakers in the world, with everything off pat to perfection, but if we do not speak from the heart we can be utterly ineffectual, for something vital will be lacking from our words. On the other hand, we may be tongue-tied, our message confused and disjointed, yet nonetheless put across the wonder of the gospel in a way that is able to change lives! As Paul continued, in his letter to the Corinthians: 'My speech and my proclamation were not with plausible words of wisdom, but with a demonstration of the Spirit and of power, so that your faith might rest not on human wisdom but on the power of God' (1 Corinthians 2:4, NRSV).

We will not get far by standing on our soapbox and quoting the Bible at people, or through reciting parrot fashion the creeds or central tenets of faith. We will get no further through engaging in complex theological debate or attempting to argue people into faith. Nor will a carefully rehearsed testimony or learned technique pay dividends if it is simply trotted out with no reference to the situation or person we are speaking to. What is needed is for us to speak, in our own words, of what Jesus means to us, what difference our faith makes to our lives, and to do that honestly, naturally and spontaneously. Many of us will feel we are not up to the job, convinced that our nervous and awkward efforts will inevitably prove fruitless. Yet if we share simply and sincerely, telling of what Christ means to us, then however ineffectual we may consider our words to be, God is able to use them and to speak to others in ways surpassing our highest expectations!

Summary

- Great oratory is a rare thing that requires special qualities, but that is not to say the rest of us cannot communicate effectively and powerfully with others.
- Unless we speak with sincerity, our words will always lack something. Conversely, we may lack any technical skills in speaking, yet still challenge people through the evident passion with which we hold our convictions.
- Here lies the secret behind the success of Peter and John's preaching in the early Church. They were not speaking because they felt they ought to, or reciting the gospel parrot fashion. Such was their faith and enthusiasm that they couldn't help but speak of it as the opportunity arose.
- The same is true of the Apostle Paul. His pharisaic education wasn't the secret behind his missionary success; rather, it was the charismatic effect of his unmistakable commitment to Christ. Compared to many, he wasn't a naturally gifted speaker and clearly at times found preaching demanding, yet spontaneous testimony to everything Jesus had accomplished in his life continually welled up within him.
- We cannot emphasise too strongly the importance of sincerity. An apparently garbled message can speak powerfully to others by God's grace. Similarly, an apparently polished sermon can leave people cold, if it does not come from the heart.

- We will communicate most effectively not through learning evangelistic techniques but through speaking honestly and openly of what Christ means to us. God is able to use a heartfelt testimony in ways that will exceed all our expectations.

Discussion

- Sincerity adds weight to our words, but that does not necessarily mean our words are right. Dictators like Adolf Hitler or Joseph Stalin passionately believed in the things they stood for, and crowds responded in turn, yet today we are appalled by their words and deeds. In what ways can we ensure that words from the heart are also words from God?

- Which people have spoken most powerfully to you? What was it about them that made you listen? In what did the strength of their message lie?

- Has the Church been guilty of regarding people as pew fodder? How can we avoid giving this impression? What should be the motivation behind all evangelism?

Prayer

Loving God,
    you do not call us all to be evangelists or preachers of your word,
    but you do call us all to be witnesses,
    telling others what Jesus has done for us.
And, through Paul, you have shown us what really counts
    if we are to do that effectively –
    not using clever words,
    not presenting carefully rehearsed arguments,
    but simply speaking openly and honestly from the heart.
Loving God,
    as we have heard, so help us to tell,
    through Jesus Christ our Lord.
Amen.

Meditation of John

We just can't help ourselves.
I know that sounds foolish,
   that we're risking our lives carrying on,
   that we'd be better off keeping our heads down,
   but it's no good:
   we have to speak,
   have to tell what God has done.
It's not that we're looking for trouble,
   don't think that;
   we value our lives as much as anyone.
It's not that we want to make a name for ourselves;
   believe me we'd both be happier out of the limelight.
And it's not that we're simply full of our own ideas,
   too self-opinionated to know when to keep quiet –
   at least, I don't think that's true, though we may be wrong.
No, the fact is we have no choice –
   despite ourselves,
   against our better judgement,
   we find the words just keep on coming.
When we're there in the synagogue, listening to the scriptures,
   we have to tell what they mean.
When we're out in the marketplace,
   the crowds thronging about us,
   we have to share the Good News.
When the lame come for healing,
   the poor for help,
   the lonely for friendship,
   and the lost for guidance,
   we have to speak of the faith we have found in Jesus,
   the way, the truth, and the life we have discovered through him.
Honestly, we've no interest in banging our own drum,
   no desire to get up on our soap-box –
   we simply have to testify to everything he's done for us,
   and everything he can do for them.

That's why we're here today waiting to appear before the Council,
   back in hot water once again and about to get another roasting.
We don't enjoy it – of course we don't –
   in fact we're terrified,
   paranoid about what they might do to us,
   unable to forget what happened to Jesus.
Oh no, we're under no illusions:
   we know full well what the cost might be
   and the prospect makes us sick with fear.
They've been lenient so far
   but they won't keep on the kid-gloves for ever.
Yet it makes no difference –
   we have to speak of what we've seen and heard.
How can we do anything less when Jesus did so much for us?
It's our duty,
   our privilege,
   our responsibility,
   the least we owe not only to *him*,
   but also to *them*.
Don't get us wrong;
   we're not going to stick our necks out for the sake of it,
   but when God gives us the words to speak
   we simply can't keep silent.

Further reading: Ephesians 3:20-21

Now to him who by his power at work within us is able to achieve inestimably more than anything we can ask or even dream of, to him be glory in the Church and in Christ Jesus in this and every generation, now and always. Amen.

Suggestions for action

Next time the opportunity presents itself to share your faith, don't think about what you *ought* to say; launch into what you *want* to say.

Closing prayer

Living God,
    you have given us glad tidings,
    good news for all people.
Save us from keeping it to ourselves.
In the name of Christ.
Amen.

Sixth week
Don't push it

Opening prayer

Lord,
    the help of the helpless,
    the hope of those past hope,
    the rescuer of the storm-tossed,
    the harbour of the voyagers,
    the healer of the sick:
    We ask you to become all things to all people,
    for you know the needs of each one.
Accept us all into your kingdom,
    making us children of light;
    and give us your peace and love,
Lord, our God.
Amen.

Liturgy of St Basil (Fourth century)

Introduction

Don't push your luck! We've probably all been given that advice on more than one occasion. Fortune seems to be smiling on us, so we take chances we would not normally take. 'Don't push your luck,' a friend warns us. Or, having got away with a mistake, we are tempted to take liberties more often, only to meet with the same warning. Not simply with luck, but in so much else, we can push things once too often, with costly results. Sometimes we need to recognise enough is enough, to understand that having done all that can be done in a situation we must leave it alone. So it is with sharing our faith. There will be times, many times, when your efforts to communicate the gospel to someone are fruitless, meeting only with stony disinterest or even hostility. It might be right to persevere for a while, or it might not, but in many circumstances it is necessary eventually to let go. We may not find that easy, especially if the person in question is someone close to us with whom we desperately want to share our faith, but the fact is that continuing to push where we are not wanted can be counterproductive, driving people away rather than encouraging them to consider the challenge of the gospel. This is not to say that we abandon hope, accepting that this person will never come to faith. It may even be that another opportunity will present itself to us later, the situation suddenly changing. We need to recognise that though we all have a part to play in witnessing to Christ, God does not depend solely on any one of us. He works through different people in a variety of ways, and just because *we* cannot get through to someone doesn't mean *he* cannot either. Share your faith, yes; tell of what Jesus means to you when and where the time seems right, but don't force your views on other people or try to coerce them into becoming Christians. Only God knows what is going on in someone else's mind, and only he, finally, has the power to change it.

Activity

Balloon challenge (see page 68).

Reading: Luke 9:1-6

Then Jesus called the twelve together and gave them power and authority over all demons and to cure diseases, and he sent them out to proclaim the kingdom of God and to heal. He said to them, 'Take nothing for your journey, no staff, nor bag, nor bread, nor money – not even an extra tunic. Whatever house you enter, stay there, and leave from there. Wherever they do not welcome you, as you are leaving that town shake the dust off your feet as a testimony against them.' They departed and went through the villages, bringing the good news and curing diseases everywhere. (*NRSV*)

Comment

There are few things worse than those who force their attentions upon us. Which of us hasn't groaned in despair as we spot a sales-man, Mormon, Jehovah's Witness or some such knocking on doors down our street? We know what they're going to say before they start to speak and we don't want to be bothered, but we know if we allow anything more than a brusque 'No, thank you', we're going to be stuck on our doorstep for an eternity listening to some pre-rehearsed spiel until we finally get the opportunity to interrupt and excuse ourselves. None of us likes being pushed to make a commitment against our wishes. We don't usually mind being asked to consider something so long as it's simply that and we're free at the end to make up our own mind, but if we're put under pressure or in any way badgered into making a decision, we understandably resent it. The result of such heavy-handed attempts to elicit a response is to make most of us automatically reject any approach without even listening to what is said.

All this may help us better to understand the words of Jesus in Luke 9:1-6, and those that follow in Chapter 10:1-11. 'Wherever they do not welcome you,' says Jesus, 'as you are leaving that town shake the dust off your feet as a testimony against them' (*NRSV*). I must say, I find those words rather difficult, for they come across as somewhat petulant, suggestive more of the actions of an angry child that fails to get its own way than a life-giving Messiah. Does Jesus really want us to stalk off if anyone refuses to listen to our message? It seems hard to believe. There are two possible explanations. It's possible that the frustration of those in the early Church is spilling over here into the narrative, their less successful attempts at mission colouring their record of Jesus' words, but it's more likely that Jesus is using the familiar rabbinical device of exaggeration to drive home the point he wants to make. In other words, he may simply be saying that we should not waste time forcing the gospel on people who do not want to hear it. The time has to come when we move on.

Why should Jesus say that? Surely with something as important as faith we have to persevere for however long it takes? No, not if it has the opposite effect to that intended. However well-intentioned, keeping on at somebody may put them off for good rather than win them over to our point of view. Is that the concern behind the words of Jesus here? Is he warning his disciples not to push for a response where they are clearly not wanted, not to spend all their time and energy trying to convert those who are either not ready for or not interested in what they have to say? That would seem to be his message not only here but in the parable of the feast recorded in Luke 14:16-24. A man extends invitations to a sumptuous meal, says Jesus, but one by one those invited offer excuses for not being able to come. What does he do? Ask them to reconsider? Send out copies of the menu in the hope it might make them think again? No, he invites others instead – the poor, crippled, blind and lame – and when there is room even after this he extends the offer still wider. The parable has its own agenda, being concerned primarily with the rejection of the gospel by the scribes, Pharisees and religious elite of his day. If these won't listen, says Jesus, others will. Yet the point is clear: don't impose your message on those who aren't interested; learn to let go.

The thrust of Jesus' words, as presented in Luke, is that those who once refuse to listen won't get another opportunity. Personally, I can't go along with that, for it runs counter to everything else in the gospel concerning the grace and mercy of God that is continually seeking us out. We must, though, take seriously his advice concerning mission. There is simply no point in ramming the gospel down people's throats; we will gain nothing by it and probably achieve quite the opposite. That is not to say we should abandon any attempt whatsoever, using a fear of rejection as an excuse to evade or ignore our call to mission, but we must offer faith freely and then leave it to people to make their own decisions. All too often, people have been pressurised, even bullied, into coming to church or making a commitment: a husband or wife, perhaps, pushed by their partner; a child, anxious to please parents; a brother or sister, doing anything for the sake of peace; a friend, fed up with being hectored. More often still, people are put off for life, wanting nothing to do with a religion that tries to force them into an unwilling surrender. In this sense, I suspect over-zealous Christians may unintentionally have done more harm over the years than the under-zealous.

Don't get me wrong. We may act from the sincerest of motives, a genuine longing to see our nearest and dearest come to faith in Christ, and we may feel that if they fail to believe we have somehow failed in our responsibilities. Yet there are times when we, like the Apostles, must learn to accept that God is able to work and speak through others apart from ourselves. There can be no hard and fast rules here. Some people need to be coaxed, challenged and gently helped to make a decision, whereas others will see that as an unwelcome intrusion. The secret of mission is being sensitive not just to when we should speak but also to when we should stop!

Summary

- Nobody likes being pushed into a commitment they are not ready to make. Attempts to do so are usually counterproductive.
- Jesus told the disciples to shake the dust off their feet when leaving a town where people refused to listen to them. His words seem to contradict the gospel's emphasis upon grace and forgiveness, but Jesus, here, was probably using the rabbinical device of hyperbole to emphasise a key point. The important lesson here is to know when to let go and move on.
- The parable of the great feast contains a similar message: if people are not willing to respond, there is no point pushing them against their wishes.
- Attempts to ram the gospel down people's throats can do more

harm than good. We may end up putting them off rather than winning them to faith in Christ. Too many people have been pressurised into making a commitment they are not ready for or have been driven away altogether from even considering what the gospel might have to say to them.

- We cannot lay down inflexible guidelines, but sometimes the most important thing in sharing our faith is to know when not to share it. God may choose to speak through people other than us; it may be we have to leave things in his hands.

Discussion

- No one has ever been argued into faith but many have been put off through those who imagine they can be. Do you think that's true or false?
- What experiences have you had of people trying to push their convictions upon you? How did you react? What harm did it do? Are there people we know who have been put off Christianity through people pressurising them?
- Are there times when we need to persevere in our witness, at least for a time? When might this be? Is there a danger we are simply refusing to let go?

Prayer

Lord Jesus Christ,
    all too often we are slow to speak for you
    and timid in our witness,
    but occasionally it is the other way round,
    there being some we care so deeply about
    that we cannot keep ourselves from sharing our faith,
    in the hope that they will share it too.
We ask for guidance in what to say and how to say it,

praying that you will speak through our witness,
flawed and hesitant though it may be,
but we pray also for sensitivity and discernment,
so that we will recognise when words serve to obstruct
rather than kindle faith.
Teach us to speak honestly of all you mean to us
but equally to trust you are able to speak
in ways we may neither realise or understand.
So, by your grace,
break down the barriers that we can unwittingly reinforce.
In your name, we ask it.
Amen.

Meditation of Simon Peter

Not listen!
Fat chance of that, I thought.
Once they heard what we had to tell them
I honestly believed we'd be fighting them off,
overwhelmed by a multitude wanting to hear more.
This was Judah, remember,
home to a people who'd waited, prayed and yearned
to see the day of the Messiah,
the dawn of God's kingdom,
and now, at last, it was among us,
in the person of Jesus,
the Prince of Peace,
the King of kings.
Of course, they'd listen –
it stood to reason –
for this was good news,
the best possible,
breathtaking,
out of this world!
Yet they didn't,

not by a long way.
A few responded, sure –
    as excited and eager as kittens,
    but for every one of them
    a hundred more didn't want to know.
'Not today,' they said,
    'too busy,
    so much to do,
    try tomorrow.'
Others simply laughed,
    yawned
    or looked the other way.
Was it fear, perhaps –
    the price that might be asked,
    the sacrifice entailed –
    or had there simply been too many would-be messiahs,
    promising much,
    delivering little?
I just don't know,
    but there was no escaping the facts –
    it was just as Jesus had warned it would be,
    many simply not interested.
I wanted to persuade them, believe me;
    to go back and explain,
    argue,
    coax,
    beg,
    for surely they'd see eventually,
    the truth finally break through?
I continue to pray for that,
    hoping and believing that one day it will happen –
    faith be born –
    but I've come to understand the point Jesus was making that day,
    or at least I think I have:
    that it's no good pushing,
    forcing yourself where you're not wanted,

throwing your pearls where no one wants to receive them.
You'll never argue anyone into the kingdom
    but you may well drive them away by trying,
    so when you've done your bit,
    shared the gospel as best you can,
    don't keep hammering away,
    battering your head against a brick wall –
    have done,
    learn to let go,
    for the rest is between them and God,
    and who knows what he may yet do!

Further reading: Luke 14:15-24

One of the dinner guests, on hearing this, said to him, 'Blessed is anyone who will eat bread in the kingdom of God!' Then Jesus said to him, 'Someone gave a great dinner and invited many. At the time for the dinner he sent his slave to say to those who had been invited, "Come; for everything is ready now." But they all alike began to make excuses. The first said to him, "I have bought a piece of land, and I must go out and see it; please accept my apologies." Another said, "I have bought five yoke of oxen, and I am going to try them out; please accept my apologies." Another said, "I have just been married, and therefore I cannot come." So the slave returned and reported this to his master. Then the owner of the house became angry and said to his slave, "Go out at once into the streets and lanes of the town and bring in the poor, the crippled, the blind, and the lame." And the slave said, "Sir, what you ordered has been done, and there is still room." Then the master said to the slave, "Go out into the roads and lanes, and compel people to come in, so that the house may be filled. For I tell you, none of those who were invited will taste my dinner."' (*NRSV*)

Suggestions for action

If there is someone you have been pressing to become a Christian, let go. Allow time and space for that person to make up his or her own mind.

Closing prayer

Lord Jesus Christ,
    teach me when to speak of you
    and when to remain silent,
    when to share my faith
    and when to leave all in your hands.
Help me to know when each time may be,
    and to respond accordingly,
    for your name's sake.
Amen.

Appendix 1
Activities

First week: No one told me

Embarrassing moments

Invite members of the group briefly to share any embarrassing or humorous moments from their experience, caused by someone not having given them information they needed to know (you may want to prime participants beforehand, so that they have time to prepare). If you have access to it, you might like to introduce this session by reading stories from Stephen Pile's *Book of Heroic Failures*. Try to limit this exercise to no more than ten minutes. Its relevance to today's theme will become clear as the session progresses.

Second week: Keep it simple

News headlines

Cut out three good-length stories from a newspaper and block out the headlines. Photocopy a sufficient number of the articles for every member of the group to have one of each. Invite participants to read them quietly and then to make up a short catchy headline that summarises the essential message of each story. Invite participants to read out their headlines and then compare these with the originals. Talk briefly together about the difficulty of isolating one key theme. What did people feel were the main difficulties in doing so? What role do headlines play? What reservations might you have concerning them?

Third week: Practising what we preach

Fishing game

Cut out paper fish-shapes, and attach a paper-clip to the head of each one. Place the shapes in buckets. Hang magnets on string from bamboo canes to serve as fishing rods. Invite participants (sitting at a suitable distance away from the buckets) to 'go fishing' and see how many of your fish they can catch. Talk afterwards about ways in which it is possible for the Church to attract people, and ask if it is realistic to talk about attractive discipleship.

Fourth week: Speaking their language

Cracking the code

Prepare a selection of encoded single-sentence messages (perhaps biblical verses on the theme of mission and evangelism) and invite the group to crack the code. Four or five such messages should be ample. You could use Morse code, sign language or a rebus as well as more traditional codes where a number or another letter is used to represent a letter of the alphabet.

Now read the following light-hearted rendition of the Lord's Prayer in the language of jargon. Make up your own version, as an example of the way *not* to communicate with people!

Our father-figure who resides in the upper-echelon domain,
may thy title always be structured to elicit a favourable response.
Reward us today, bread-wise,
and minimise our unfavourable self-concept,
resulting from credit over-extension,
as we will strive to practise reciprocal procedures.
And channel us, not into temptation-inducing areas,
but provide us with security from situations
not conducive to moral enrichment.
For thine is the position of maximum achievement
in the power structure,
not to mention the prestige-attainment factor that never terminates.

(Tom Dodge, 'What If an Educator Had Written "The Lord's Prayer"', *English Journal*, January 1971)

Talk briefly together about the jargon we use as Christians. Identify terminology that might mean little or nothing to a non-Christian.

Fifth week: Words from the heart

Immortal lines

Some words have spoken so powerfully that they have gone down in history. Most of us will be able to recognise them, and some may even know them word for word. Below are extracts from ten speeches, plays or poems, each of which represent words from the heart. See if you can complete them, and identify the source of each.

1. I know I have the body of a weak and feeble woman,
2. We shall fight on the beaches, we shall fight on the landing grounds,
3. Never in the field of human conflict
4. Out, damned spot!
5. I have a dream that my four little children will one day live in a nation where they will not be judged by the colour of their skin
6. I just want to do God's will. And he's allowed me to go up the mountain.
7. O Romeo, Romeo!
8. They shall not grow old, as we that are left grow old.
9. In Flanders fields the poppies blow
10. My God, my God,

Discuss briefly together what gives these words their power. What is it about them that speaks to us? Why are they remembered by so many?

Sixth week: Don't push it

Balloon challenge

Distribute balloons among group members, challenging them to blow as much air into them as possible before tying a knot in them. The aim is to see who can make the biggest balloon! Afterwards, briefly discuss what happened. Did people keep on blowing until their balloon burst? Did they inflate them so much that it was impossible to tie a knot? Or did they err on the side of caution? Relate this to sharing our faith and knowing when it is time to stop. Can we end up doing more harm than good if we fail to recognise people will only take so much?

Appendix 2

Answers

Fifth week: Words from the heart

1. I know I have the body of a weak and feeble woman, **but I have the heart and stomach of a king, and of a king of England too.**
(Queen Elizabeth I)

2. We shall fight on the beaches, we shall fight on the landing grounds, **we shall fight in the fields and in the streets, we shall fight in the hills; we shall never surrender.**
(Winston Churchill)

3. Never in the field of human conflict **was so much owed by so many to so few.**
(Winston Churchill)

4. Out, damned spot! **out, I say!**
(words of Lady Macbeth in *Macbeth*, by William Shakespeare)

5. I have a dream that my four little children will one day live in a nation where they will not be judged by the colour of their skin **but by the content of their character.**
(Martin Luther King)

6. I just want to do God's will. And he's allowed me to go up the mountain.
And I've looked over, and I've seen the promised land.
(Martin Luther King)

7. O Romeo, Romeo! **wherefore art thou, Romeo?**
(words of Juliet in *Romeo and Juliet*, by William Shakespeare)

8. They shall not grow old, as we that are left grow old.
   Age shall not weary them, nor the years condemn.
   At the going down of the sun and in the morning
   we will remember them.
   (from the poem 'For the Fallen', by Laurence Binyon)

9. In Flanders fields the poppies blow
   between the crosses, row on row,
   that mark our place; and in the sky
   the larks, still bravely singing, fly
   scarce heard amid the guns below.
   (from the poem 'In Flanders Fields', by John McCrae)

10. My God, my God, **why hast thou forsaken me?**
    (Matthew 27:46, *AV*)

Also in this series:
Living with questions – exploring faith and doubt
Paul – the man and the mission
Prayer – the fundamental questions
Unsung gifts – the Spirit at work in the New Testament
Love – the key to it all
Discipleship – the journey of faith
Women of faith – what they teach us

Also by Nick Fawcett:
No ordinary man (books 1 and 2)
Resources for reflective worship on the person of Jesus

The unfolding story
Resources for reflective worship on the Old Testament

Grappling with God (books 1-4)
Old Testament studies for personal and small-group use

To put it another way
Resources for reflective worship on the Parables

Are you listening?
Honest prayers about life

Prayers for all seasons (books 1 and 2)
A comprehensive resource for public worship

Getting it across
One hundred talks for family worship

Decisions, decisions
A Lent study course

Promises, promises
An Advent study course

Daily prayer
A book of daily devotions

All the above titles are available from your local Christian bookshop
or direct from Kevin Mayhew Ltd, telephone 01449 737978,
fax: 01449 737834, email: sales@kevinmayhewltd.com